CW0055476Ø

HARRY'S ABC of Mixing Cocktails

369
Famous Cocktails
by
HARRY MacELHONE
with new material by
ANDREW MacELHONE
and
DUNCAN MacELHONE

SOUVENIR PRESS

First published 1919
Second edition, with additional material,
published 1986 by Souvenir Press Ltd.,
43 Great Russell Street, London WC1B 3PA
and simultaneously in Canada

Reprinted 1986, 1988, 1990, 1992, 1993
New edition, revised and enlarged, published 1996

ISBN 0 285 63358 9

Typeset by Galleon Typesetting, Ipswich
Printed in Great Britain by
St Edmundsbury Press Ltd, Bury St Edmunds, Suffolk
Bound by Hunter & Foulis, Edinburgh

*This book is respectfully dedicated
to all past, present, and future
INTERNATIONAL BARFLIES*

THE CRADLE OF
FAMOUS COCKTAILS

This ABC of Mixing Cocktails was written by my father, Harry MacElhone, while he was still at Ciro's Club in London in 1919.

After he took over 'Sank Roo Doe Noo' in Paris, it was re-edited every year until 1939.

I hope that this new edition will interest and help all the young bartenders who are starting out in the profession and will be a useful handbook for those who enjoy mixing cocktails at home.

Harry's Hints to Bartenders have never been improved on, also his Arrangement of a Bar.

New products and new cocktails have been brought into this edition, but one must remember that there will never again be another Dry Martini invented.

Andy MacElhone

A FEW POINTS OF INTEREST
AT 'SANK ROO DOE NOO'

It was in 1911 that the popular and successful jockey Tod Sloan decided to go into partnership with a New Yorker named Clancey, to open a saloon in Paris that would be called the *New York Bar*. The location chosen was 5 rue Daunou in the Opera district, between the rue de la Paix and the avenue de l'Opera.

Clancey, who already owned a bar in New York, dismantled its counter and its walls' mahogany wood panelling and had them shipped to Paris. Meanwhile, Tod Sloan got in touch with one of the few bartenders of that period, Harry MacElhone, a Scot from Dundee, and asked him to come and operate behind the bar for the opening, which took place on Thanksgiving Day of that year.

Initially the bar became the natural meeting place of the racing crowd of that period, and of those taking the European grand tour. When the dark days of 1914 came along, it was the focus of relaxation for the American Volunteers of the Lafayette Escadrille and their famous French companions, such as Guynemer and other gallant men; the American Field Service made it its unofficial HQ.

Harry, meanwhile, had left for New York where, in 1912, he tended bar at the Plaza Hotel. When the war broke out he made his way back to Europe and volunteered for the Royal Naval Air Service. The year 1919 saw him out of the Force and working at Ciro's Club in London, then the most fashionable night spot in Europe. After a few years at Ciro's, he decided to return to Paris and in 1923 took over the New York Bar and added his name to it as a prefix. So the first Harry's Bar came into existence.

This was also the beginning of the roaring Twenties, and they hit the New York Bar with fury. Young Scott Fitzgerald chewed on his first Paris dry martini olive there; Gershwin pounded its 'Downstairs Room' piano to pieces putting together his *American in Paris*; Hemingway repaired to it after his friendly boxing bouts at the Montmartre Sportif, where Harry acted as his towel holder; the Dolly Sisters paraded their hats there, and the young Prince of Wales (later the Duke of Windsor) came in to have one for the road. Fanny Ward and her husband held court in the champagne only 'Downstairs Room' where Tommy Lyman and Roy Barton of 'Momartre Rose' fame gave out with the vocal chords and the piano.

In 1924 O.O. McIntyre and Harry formed the International BarFlies which, in their words, was to be a 'secret and fraternal organisation devoted to the uplift and downfall of serious drinkers'. A set of rules was made, an insignia picturing a fly on a cube of sugar was designed and a secret handshake was invented. It was an immediate success and before long Fly Traps were established all around the world. The IBF has not stopped buzzing since. There are now more than 134 traps ranging from Paris to Munich by way of London, Rome, Madrid, Montreux, Salzburg, and all points East and West.

The first Hot Dog served in France was pushed across the counter at Harry's Bar in 1925. It was the year when the immortal Sparrow Robertson made his appearance in France, and particularly at Harry's which became his favourite 'Drink

Emporium'. This was also the year when such people as Suzanne Lenglen, Jack Dempsey, Primo Carnera, Tilden, Sinclair Lewis, Ramon Novarro, Captain Noville (of South Pole fame) Rockne and Carpentier came into the bar. Many famous people came in, and many famous drinks were invented: already, in 1921, the birth of the Bloody Mary had taken place, invented by Pete Petiot, who was then tending bar at 5 rue Daunou; Harry's White Lady, Side Car, and many others also came into being.

The Crash, the Depression, the tumbling rate of the $ took their toll. Harry's New York Bar kept on going—maybe with a little difficulty, but who didn't in those days? The World's Fair of 1937 in Paris saw it in the pink again.

The year 1939 at first brought with it all the rediscovered glamour of uniforms; once again the American Field Service made an appearance, together with the Iroquois Ambulance Corps, Teddy Schultz's Polish-American Ambulance Unit, and many of the war correspondents like Robert Casey, Eric Baume (from Australia), Quentin Reynolds, R. Packard and all the other gifted pen wielders who kept the world informed of the news. The clouds grew darker and finally the unbelievable happened: Paris was occupied. Harry left for London by way of Bordeaux, a few steps ahead of the advancing German army. A few months later *Harry's Bar* was functioning again, open to the public but taken over as an enemy property business by the German Occupation Forces. A manager was put in charge and the Bar kept going. It has been said that it was one of the few places where one could speak English during the Occupation, since most of the German officers patronising the Bar at rare intervals were homesick ex-Chicagoans, or pre-war German students of Oxford, Harvard or

Cambridge. During those sombre days Harry was at the Café de Paris in London, where he tended bar with his son Andy until the place was blown to bits by the direct hit of a 500 lb bomb which left 80 dead and more than 120 wounded. Having escaped that, Harry and Andy went to tend bar at the new Rivoli Bar of the Ritz Hotel, where Harry remained until April 1945.

In 1944, a few days after the liberation of Paris, came the muted reopening of *Harry's Bar* with Harry *in absentia*. Charlie the French bartender with the Hoboken accent, and Robert the waiter (just out of the Army) reopened—or rather took back—Harry's New York Bar. The cellars were bare, but the gaiety and cheerfulness of the past were still there. So was that old friend Ernest Hemingway, and so many others.

On 2 April, 1945, Harry was one of the first five civilians allowed to travel between England and France on purely personal business. Things were still grim in Paris—rationing, electricity power cuts, lack of fuel and bread—but gradually things returned to normal. Paris regained its place in the sun and *Harry's Bar* its pre-war swing. Slowly the shelves began to be refilled with gleaming bottles of Highland brew. Beer was again on tap and rolls could be obtained for the hot dogs.

Andy came back in 1947 after six years in the British Army, now sporting a big black moustache behind the bar. Harry was able to find his favourite brand of cigar and was again the affable host he knew so well how to be. As in the old days, *Harry's New York Bar* was now a thriving place, a 'home from home'.

Once more collegiates tried to break the world's beer drinking record, held since 1932 by J.H. Cochrane, then of Princeton, who had quaffed 2 litres or 2 and $\frac{1}{10}$ quarts in the astonishing time of 11 seconds.

The French clientele, which had always been limited, was beginning to increase and English ceased to be the only language spoken. In fact Harry's soon became the rendezvous of French intellectuals, with such people as Marcel Achard, Jean-Paul Sartre, Jacques Prevert, Henri Jeanson, Pierre Kast, Simone de Beauvoir and Kleber-Haedens.

In June 1958 Harry quietly passed away. Although he had more or less retired five years before, his presence was very strongly felt, and his loss still more. His friends, the newsmen the world over, paid him many tributes in the press; among them the editorial of the *New York Herald Tribune* was one of the most moving.

Despite the prevailing sadness, according to Harry's wishes the Bar did not close even for a day. Andy took over the succession and *Sank Roo Doe Noo* kept going. The dry martinis were the driest in town, the Mint Juleps the tallest, and with over 49 brands of Highland brew to choose from, plus some specially shipped barrels of malt whisky, the mahogany bar counter still saw some of the most distinguished and intelligent elbows in the world—those of James Jones, Pierre Brasseur, Glenn Ford, Jeanne Moreau, Thornton Wilder, Brendan Behan, Marlene Dietrich, François Perrier, Gene Kelly, Marguerite Duras of *Hiroshima mon Amour* fame, and many others of the world of the cinema and intellectual life, plus all the world's travellers, IBF Gourmets and *bon vivants* who had made a habit of dropping in at *Sank Roo Doe Noo*.

In the summer of 1959, for the last time, our

old friend Ernest Hemingway paid a visit to *Sank Roo Doe Noo*. His first one had been back in 1918 on his way to Italy, when he had stayed at a small hotel not far from the Madeleine church; his next drink at *Harry's* was in 1923, and from then on he was a constant visitor both at the Bar and at Harry's private home, in Chatou just outside Paris.

The US Presidential Election in November 1960 drew considerable attention. *Harry's Bar* Straw Vote, which had been instituted by Harry as far back as 1924, had its usual success and brought great crowds—so many that the Police had to close the rue Daunou to traffic; it has been the same at every election since then.

During the month of May 1968, James Jones found it necessary to open his own private *Harry's Bar*, within his Left Bank apartment in Paris, due to difficulties in crossing the Seine at the time.

Then, in 1974, after a two-year search, Andy finally found premises in Munich and opened *Harry's Bar* at Falkensturmstrasse 9. A novice to the profession, Bill Deck from Pennsylvania but a long-time Munich resident, started operations under Paris's stewardship. Great care and attention were given to reproducing the décor of the original *Harry's Bar*—vintage mahogany for the same-shape bar counter, hard-to-get 1900 lampshades and made-to-measure bar-stools. An announcement was even placed in the *Herald Tribune* to try to find a phonetic equivalent of *Sank Roo Doe Noo* and a case of Champagne was offered as a reward, but this was to no avail.

In 1975 *Harry's Bar* Paris was asked to participate in an 'April in Paris' show at the Hong Kong Hilton Hotel, where the Grill Room was done up in the typical *Harry's* decoration, with proper cocktail formulas. This was so well received by the local International BarFlies that April 1976 saw *Harry's Bar* once more happily installed in Hong Kong.

Meanwhile, in 1977, *Harry's* was asked to cater to 4,600 guests of Chancellor Helmut Schmidt for the Bundeskanzlerfest in Bonn. *Harry's Bar* atmosphere was carefully reproduced by the Bonn Opera decorators. The following year the Bar was again in Bonn for the Fest, but this time we went one better by having a champagne-fountain built, consisting of more than 225 hollow-stem champagne glasses, one over the other. The stems were filled with Cherry Brandy, so that when the Champagne Magnums were sabre-cut opened and poured, the fountain became a wonderful light pink colour.

In 1979 a French mountaineering expedition set off to climb the peak of K2 in the Himalayas. Being good and true IBFs, they set up a *Harry's Bar* at their base camp; the one near the summit was blown away by the prevailing winds.

The years 1980 and 1981 were spent preparing for the Paris *Harry's* seventieth anniversary and Munich's seventh. In December 1981 the third *Harry's Bar* was opened aboard a new German luxury liner, MS *Astor*. Naturally an Astor Cocktail was created for the world's first floating *Harry's*. In 1982 MS *Astor* entered the Port of New York for the first time on one of its cruises, and a grand party took place on board to celebrate the return of *Harry's New York Bar* to its original home of 71 years ago. Two of Hemingway's sons, Jack and Patrick, joined the Paris and Munich clients to make merry.

In 1983, after graduating from Georgetown University class of '77, and following a stint in banking and international finance, Duncan

14

MacElhone, grandson of Harry, came to join the Bar, to become the third generation of MacElhones to look after the welfare of its clients. The following year saw the opening of a new *Harry's Bar*—the first one in Switzerland—at the Montreux Palace on the shores of Lac Leman in Montreux. In Paris, the Straw Vote went off in great style and was proved right once again: Reagan was the winner both in the US and Paris.

In 1986, we celebrated our 75th Anniversary. The year kicked off with the launching of the Liberty Cocktail (recipe by Duncan) in co-operation with the Franco-American Committee for the Restoration of the Statue of Liberty. This cocktail was served at the Bar until the 4th of July, with a contribution to the Committee for each cocktail sold.

Ten years after its last visit, *Harry's Bar* once again winged its way to Hong Kong where the Hong Kong Hilton Hotel gave it another marvellous welcome.

As on its 50th anniversary, various events took place, such as the revival of a typical New York free lunch counter, and at certain times the use of 1911 prices. Thanksgiving Day saw our first evening of birthday celebrations from 9 pm to 4 am, complete with a birthday cake with 75 candles. The following Sunday we annexed the Rue Daunou and held a twelve-hour party.

In May 1987 *Harry's* again celebrated April in Paris at the Hong Kong Hilton. In June, 25 World War I veterans, in France to celebrate the seventieth anniversary of the USA entry into the War, gathered at *Harry's* for a champagne party, having received the French Legion of Honour that morning.

In 1988 a *Harry's Bar* was opened in the new Grand Hotel Esplanade situated on Lützowufer in Berlin. The hotel and the bar are a tribute to German modern architectural design and a true statement from the owners Messrs. Hauert and Otrember. Located a stone's throw away from the Philharmonic, the National Gallery, the State Library and the Bauhaus Archives, it puts *Harry's* right on spot in this thriving city.

In 1990 *Harry's* boarded Hapag-Lloyd's, Bremen registry, luxury liner MS *Europa* on which it has already sailed the seven seas on such memorable journeys as the 1994 Hong Kong to Genoa passage.

In the meantime, in 1991, *Harry's* of the Montreux Palace launched the first annual 'Harry's Ski Cup' in nearby Morgin, an event which grows yearly in attendance and prizes. In 1992 *Harry's* participants in the 16th Straw Vote in Paris, Munich and Berlin proved to be right again in selecting the US President-to-be.

The spring of 1995 saw the arrival of *Harry's* in Hanover within the refitted Pelikan pen factory, now reborn as the Seidler Hotel Pelikan.

All branches of *Harry's Bar* look forward to welcoming all International BarFlies and old and new friends with *Harry's* usual cocktails and services. See you there soon . . .

In 1997 the International BarFlies will issue new membership cards to all holders and descendants of IBFs. As usual your suggestions for new BarFly Trap Establishments worldwide are welcome (International BarFlies, World Headquarters, 5 rue Daunou, Paris 75002, France).

Since Harry MacElhone took over *Sank Roo Doe Noo* in Paris, many have taken advantage of *Harry's Bar*'s name and reputation. One of the first to do so was in Venice in 1931, with Harry's agreement; another in Florence, with Andy's OK, in 1953. Quite a few others have sprung up, in places as far apart as Guadalahara, London, the Philippines, New York, Japan, Los Angeles, etc. . . .

We are highly honoured about all this, but at times we cannot help but feel they could have used a little imagination, and called their establishments Giuseppe's or Nino's or Hokaro's . . . Still, it's a great tribute to the first *Harry's* and to Harry himself.

And, as this century draws to a close, we look forward to our 85th Anniversary on Thanksgiving Day 1996 as a time to thank you: our customers and friends and all IBFs for having made all the good times possible and for having stood by us in hardship. A short while before that, our 17th Straw Vote will have been tallied and the official results followed closely using today's state of the art communication tools, as has been the custom since it was first launched by Harry in 1924; results came to *Sank Roo Doe Noo* by the telegraph in those days.

As on our 50th and 75th anniversaries, we say today, looking forward to our hundredth in the twenty-first century: We hope that here at *Harry's Bar* over these years, we have made more friends than foes, and raise our glasses to say:

CHEERS!

Andy and Duncan MacElhone

Harry's New York Bar
5 rue Daunou,
Paris 75002,
France

Harry's New York Bar
MS *Europa*,
Bremen,
and at sea

Harry's New York Bar
Montreux Palace,
Montreux,
Switzerland

Harry's New York Bar
Grand Hotel Esplanade,
Lützowufer 15,
Berlin,
Germany

Harry's Bar
Seidler Hotel Pelikan,
Podbeilskistrasse 145,
Hanover,
Germany

Licensing, Franchising handled by:
Harry's Bar sa,
8 Rue St Léger,
Geneva,
Switzerland

The text on the following pages was written
by Harry MacElhone for the original edition
of *Harry's ABC of Mixing Cocktails*,
published in 1919.

HARRY'S
ABC OF MIXING COCKTAILS

As there has been such a great demand for my
ABC of Mixing Cocktails since I left Ciro's,
London, to open a place of my own in Paris,
known far and wide as Harry's New York Bar,
5 rue Daunou, Paris, in this new edition I have
added all the latest cocktails; at the same time, as
I am now a proprietor, there are a few things
which may be of some service to those pushing
young men who want to branch out themselves.
If you want to make your business successful,
you must obtain, right from the start, the best
staff possible, for the better your assistants, the
more friends you will make, and the better
you will be able to conduct your business;
having secured your employees, pay them well,
and treat them as they ought to be treated—
politely—and in that way set them a good
example.

Don't ignore the people who work for you;
that will be the most serious mistake you can
make. Treat them kindly and encourage them to
take an interest in your business, for no man can
succeed with employees who fail to interest
themselves in *his* interests, or you may be carry-
ing dead wood in your pay roll and you are
bound to suffer for it. It is a fact that when the
employees are not treated right, the proprietor

acting harshly or with an overbearing manner, never having a good word for anyone, will fail to make a success; for his employees, instead of caring for his interests, will be antagonistic to him, caring little whether his business runs down or not. Employers and employees should be in harmony with one another, in every direction the proprietor looking upon his assistants as friends, regarding them with a family feeling, while they should have the proper respect for him as an authorised manager, but with no fear, and certainly with no idea of treating him familiarly.

Another item to which you should pay particular attention is to let your employees go off duty at the hours designated, and not detain them. The employees, too, are to be just as precise in going to work at the exact minute specified; there should be a perfect system of working hours, the time of which is not to be disregarded by either party. If business is a success it is advisable to give an occasional extra holiday, in proper proportion, providing the assistant is worthy, from long and earnest service; or if possible, in the summer season, to let the employees have it at different times, though this is naturally a difficult matter in our line of business. And if the proprietor is successful he should not display a pride in his own rise, and imagine it is all the result of his own brilliant mind, claiming entire credit for his financial progress, but acknowledge his indebtedness to his helpers, for without their assistance he would not have made such a rapid advance on the ladder of success. Give encouragement where it is due, but do not let them think that it is by their efforts alone your business has prospered, for if you flatter them too much, you can easily spoil the best of men in your employ.

Treat everyone fairly and justly and have no favourites; one man's money is, all things considered, as good as another's, providing he is not so intoxicated that he should be refused. And here is where the good saloon-keeper's best judgement comes into play: he should know how to treat the man who has drunk too much, and he should be careful not to abuse him. There are times when money laid on the bar should not be accepted; it is a difficult matter to lay down rules for such cases, in fact it is impossible; consider if you like that you are in business for the sake of money, but not at the expense of your reputation. Have no special bottles for special customers, don't spoil your trade by giving away too much or treating too often, but be fair and just, give value for money received, and you will find it the surest and most satisfactory way to prosperity.

Harry MacElhone

ARRANGEMENT OF A BAR

The practical proprietor who expects the best possible results from his bartenders will pay especial attention to the making and arrangement of what is known as the working bench, which is really one of the most important fixtures in a bar. I have seen many a handsome establishment here and abroad which has a bench that hampers and impedes the work of a good barman. This is a place in the making of which no reasonable expense should be spared. It should be lined with tinned copper. The plumbing should be open and sanitary. The sink for water should be made with rounded edges, so as to make cleaning a simple matter. The liquor box should be arranged as in the plan below, with at least nine metal tubes to contain the following bottles: 1 gin, 1 French

Plan of working bench underneath bar counter

vermouth, 1 Italian vermouth, 1 rye whiskey, 1 Scotch, 1 bottle orange juice, 1 bottle lemon juice, 2 syphons. The bottles should fit freely in the tubes up to the neck. The ice box, which is to hold the broken ice, should have a false bottom of perforated wood, as an ice pick, even in the hands of a careful man, is liable to do a lot of damage. Everything below the bench should be open, and a well-made box for empty bottles kept where it can be conveniently reached. The floor should be kept clean and drained, and covered with slat work. The run behind the average bar is usually unclean and damp, and there is no excuse for such a condition of affairs, which is caused by either poor drainage or carelessness on the part of the bartender.

If the space behind the under part of the bar is dark it should be lighted artificially, and the extra expense will be more than made up by the saving resulting from fewer breakages. The bench facing should be of corrugated metal with a pitch sufficient to make drainage an easy matter. Don't forget to have the receptacle for powdered sugar and your fruits, etc., in a place that will be convenient to reach as well as dry.

When mixing, the wisest plan for the novice is to pour ingredients in the shaker first and afterwards add the ice, as then a mistake can easily be rectified. Great care should be taken to avoid using snowy ice, which dissolves too quickly and gives the beverage a watery flavour. As to stirring a cocktail, this is done in a large bar glass (pint size) by stirring briskly with a long bar spoon. This practice was not in much use in New York just before America went dry, but in fact it is essential to stir a cocktail when you are mixing drinks containing an effervescent liquid, and advisable when using clear ingredients. The shaker is used when mixing fruit juices or cordials.

TENDING BAR

Bartending may, to the man who knows nothing about it, seem a very simple matter; but like everything else it is a business, and requires considerable study to become an expert. Of course this is leaving the mixing of drinks entirely out of consideration; what is referred to now is the act of waiting upon a customer so that there will be no hitch of any kind nor any misunderstanding. The successful barman of today is alert, bright, cheerful, courteous, speaks when spoken to, or only so far as a query concerning the drink, is clean and neat in dress and makes no unnecessary display of jewellery.

To be abrupt, insolent, to talk too much, or to be slovenly in appearance is a positive detriment, and is inexcusable.

When mixed drinks are called for, they should be mixed above the counter and in full view of the customer. There should be no mistakes and no accidents, as at that particular time they are inexcusable; everything should be done neatly and with despatch. Nine men out of ten should be served quickly and without any unnecessary fuss. Remember that perfect service is half the game; after the drinks have been served and paid for and change delivered, the debris should be immediately cleared away and the bar wiped dry. Bear in mind that a place for everything will save a lot of time, trouble and confusion, especially behind the bar, and no rush should interfere with this system. This especially applies to the working bench. That subject has already been touched on, but too much cannot be said on it, as it is of immense importance.

The really good bartender is the man who has the ability of suiting and pleasing his customer; who recognises that there are several grades of cocktails: mild, medium and strong, and observes any suggestions which may be made concerning them. There are a certain number of men behind the bar who think they know it all, and who turn out drinks irrespective of the individual taste of the men most to be considered—those who pay for them and drink them. It will not take a good bartender long to work up a big personal following which may be of great value to him later on if he has a place of his own.

HINTS TO BARTENDERS

While there are really few rules by which a bartender may be governed, yet the new man in the business ought to have some sort of a guide, so that he can conduct himself in a manner that will do credit to the establishment and give satisfaction to the customer. He should be polite, prompt, and attentive at all times, and never lose his temper under any circumstances. It is important that he should always be cheerful and answer all questions put to him in as intelligent a manner as possible. He should be cheerful and amicable at all times, and try to memorise his clients' names, as it always pleases the clients when he remembers them and their particular kind of beverage.

Above all things, it is necessary that he should be well and neatly dressed, without show, and while on the subject of dressing, it might as well be mentioned that nothing is better or more appropriate than a white bar-jacket and white apron, spotlessly clean. Assume, now, that a customer has stepped up to the bar. Inquire as to his wants. If it is a mixed drink prepare it above the counter as expeditiously as possible. Do all the work in plain view, for there is nothing to conceal, and do it as it ought to be done, without any attempt at unusual elaboration. Above all things be neat. See that the glasses are brightly polished and that everything that is used to prepare the drink is perfectly clean. If there is no rush, attend to the customer until he has finished drinking and left the bar. Then the bar should be immediately and thoroughly cleaned and it will not have the untidy and sloppy appearance for which too many places are noted. Also clean the glasses and put them back where they belong, so as to have them ready for the next time they are used. During your daily work don't overlook the bar bench, but keep it neat and in good working order. Too much attention cannot be paid to this part of the bar, and a good bartender can always be told by the way his bench looks.

When you are behind the bar don't smoke. Don't, under any circumstances, drink with customers while on duty. When your work for the day is finished don't hang around; get out at once. Don't shake dice or play games of chance with customers.

Familiarity breeds contempt. Don't get too chummy with people on short notice. Look out for the hangers-on. They are always knockers. Let all customers have all the arguments among themselves; a good listener is a wise man. Therefore do your work conscientiously, holding the minor details of each day's business well in hand, and do not invent new drinks (which are often purely revamped old ones) unless you really have discovered something of intrinsic merit. In this age of great progress and many kinds of drinks it seems to have become the mission of almost every dilettante to provide a new drink for every other dilettante, and the result is that we are literally entangled in meshes of inextricable complications. The experienced bartender is heart-sick, the novice is dismayed. It is safe to state that not one drinker out of 100,000 could, for a lottery grand prize, enumerate fifty modern drinks outside of the straight drinks, but do not be dismayed or discouraged. This little volume contains all the drinks that you will ever have occasion to use;

but they are here if needed, and easy to refer to at a second's notice. After all, most of these modern drinks outside of the old standards are only slight variations from the parent mixture, and are obtained by the addition of a dash of this and a dash of that, etc., and they are ephemeral. And lastly, when looking for a change of jobs, don't forget cheap bartenders are of very little use, and there is no reason why a man ought to be cheap. As a rule, a cheap man is worthless except for a cheap place.

Harry MacElhone

Abyssinia Cocktail

⅓ Crème de Cacao, ⅓ Cognac, ⅓ Grapefruit Juice. Shake and strain.

Adonis Cocktail

1 dash of Orange Bitters, ⅓ Sherry, ⅔ Sweet Vermouth. Stir and strain.

After All

⅓ Calvados, ⅓ Peach Brandy, ⅓ Lemon Juice. Shake and strain.

Alaska Cocktail

⅓ Yellow Chartreuse, ⅔ Gin. Stir and strain.

Alexander Cocktail

⅓ Crème de Cacao, ⅓ Cognac, ⅓ fresh cream. Shake and strain.

Alfonso Cocktail

Directly in champagne glass: ice-cube, lump of sugar impregnated Angostura, ¼ of glass with Dubonnet. Fill remainder with Champagne, squeeze lemon peel, stir slightly.

This cocktail was very popular in Deauville, in 1922, during the King of Spain's visit to this fashionable Normandy resort.

Algonquin

½ Rye Whiskey, ¼ Martini Dry Vermouth, ¼ Pineapple Juice. Shake and strain.

Alligator

⅔ Gin, ⅓ Kiwi Liqueur, 1 dash Lemon Juice.
Stir and strain.
(Recipe: Guy Lacouchie, Paris, 1990.)

Aloha

³⁄₁₀ White Rum, ²⁄₁₀ Vanilla 'Bourbon' Liqueur,
¹⁄₁₀ Amaretto, ²⁄₁₀ Orange Juice, ²⁄₁₀ fresh cream.
Shake well and strain.
(Recipe: Jean-Marc Vettesi, Paris, 1994.)

American Beauty

In large tumbler: ice, 1 teaspoonful of Crème de
Menthe; then in shaker: ⅙ Orange Juice, ⅙
Grenadine, ⅓ Dry Vermouth, ⅓ Cognac. Shake
and pour in tumbler, top with a little Port Wine,
decorate with sprig of fresh mint, serve with
straw.

American MaiTai

²⁄₁₀ Bourbon, ¹⁄₁₀ Triple Sec, ¹⁄₁₀ fresh Lime Juice,
⁴⁄₁₀ Pineapple Juice, 1 dash Almond Syrup.
Shake well and strain. Decorate with Pineapple
and Maraschino Cherry.
(Recipe: Peter Kallweit, Hamburg, 1992.)

Americano

In short tumbler: ice, ⅓ Campari, ⅓ Dry Vermouth, ⅓ Sweet Vermouth, ½ slice of lemon.
Fill with Soda Water.

Angel's Kiss

Into liqueur-glass: ¾ Crème de Cacao, then float
¼ fresh cream on top.

Apotheke Cocktail

⅓ Fernet Branca, ⅓ Crème de Menthe, ⅓ Carpano. Shake well and strain.

Apple Jack Cocktail

⅔ Apple Jack, ⅙ Grenadine, ⅙ Lemon Juice. Shake and strain.

Aramis

In shaker: ice, ⅓ Armagnac, ⅓ Lemon Juice, ⅓ Kibowi. Shake and strain.
(Recipe: Duncan MacElhone, Harry's Bar, Paris, 1985.)

Astor Cocktail

1 dash of Angostura, ¼ Southern Comfort, ¼ Cointreau, ¼ Orange Juice, ¼ Rose's Lime. Shake and strain in champagne glass. Fill with Champagne, decorate with cherry.
(Recipe: Harry's Bar, Munich, 1981.)

Athos

In mixing glass: ice, 2 dashes of Angostura, ⅔ Armagnac, ⅓ Sweet Martini Vermouth. Stir and strain in cocktail glass.

Attack Cocktail

½ Calvados, ¼ Sherry, ¼ Cognac, 1 dash of Anis, 3 dashes of Grenadine, 1 dash of Angostura. Shake and strain. ,
(Recipe: Johnny's Bar, Paris, 1930.)

B 52

⅓ Bailey's, ⅓ Cognac, ⅓ Coffee Liqueur. Shake, strain and serve with freshly ground Nutmeg atop.

Bacardi Cocktail

⅔ Bacardi Rum, ⅙ Gin, ⅙ Lime or Lemon Juice, 2 dashes of Grenadine. Shake and strain.

Badida Cocktail

In old-fashioned glass: ice, liquid honey (1 or 2 teaspoonfuls), ⅓ fresh Lime Juice, ⅔ Pitu. Stir well and serve.

Baja

⅓ Anejo Tequila, ⅓ Banana Liqueur, ⅙ Banana Juice, ⅙ Lime Juice.
(Recipe: Duncan MacElhone, Paris, 1992.)

Balalaika Cocktail

⅓ Vodka, ⅓ Cointreau, ⅓ Lemon Juice. Shake and strain.

Bamboo Cocktail

1 dash of Orange Bitters, ½ wine glass of Sherry, ½ wine glass of Dry Vermouth. Stir well and strain in wine glass, squeeze lemon peel.
(Recipe: Charlie Mahoney, Hoffman House, New York, 1910.)

Banana Boat

⅓ Dark Rum, ⅙ Passoa, ⅓ Banana Juice, ⅙ Lemon Juice. Shake well and strain.
(Recipe: Metaff, Montreux, 1988.)

Bellini 'de Luxe'

2/6 Cognac vsop, 2/6 Peach Liqueur, 2/6 Peach Juice, 2 dashes Lemon Juice. Shake well and strain into a rock glass. Top off with Champagne. *(Recipe: Patrick Foynard, Paris, 1988.)*

Bernice Cocktail

1/3 Vodka, 1/3 Galliano, 1/3 Lime Juice. Shake and strain.
(Recipe: C.S. Berner, Tail O' the Cock, Los Angeles, 1950.)

Between the Sheets

1/3 Cognac, 1/3 Cointreau, 1/3 Bacardi, 2 dashes of Lemon Juice. Shake and strain.

Bicycle

In tumbler on ice: 1/4 Cassis, 1/4 Noilly Prat. Finish off with 1/2 Champagne.

Bijou Cocktail

1 dash of Orange Bitters, 1/3 Green Chartreuse, 1/3 Sweet Vermouth, 1/3 Gin. Stir and strain, add an olive.
(Recipe: Harry Johnson, New Orleans.)

Black Mischief

1/3 Kahlua, 2/3 Cognac. Serve very hot, with a little water, in a short tumbler; decorate with a cinnamon stick.
(Recipe: Duncan MacElhone, Harry's Bar, Paris.)

Black Russian Cocktail

½ Vodka, ½ Tia Maria. Either directly on the rocks or shake and strain.

Black Velvet

In large champagne glass: ½ Champagne, ½ Guinness.

Blackthorn Cocktail

2 dashes of Angostura, 3 dashes of Anis, ½ Irish Whiskey, ½ Dry Vermouth. Stir and strain.

Block and Fall Cocktail

⅙ Anis, ⅙ Calvados, ⅓ Cognac, ⅓ Cointreau. Shake and strain.
(Recipe: T. Van Dycke at Ciro's Club, Deauville, 1924.)

Bloodhound Cocktail

⅓ Gin, ⅓ Dry Vermouth, ⅓ Sweet Vermouth, 2 or 3 fresh strawberries. Shake well and strain. (This cocktail was introduced to London by the Duke of Manchester in the Twenties.)

Bloody Bull

⅓ Tequila, ⅓ Beef Broth, ⅓ Tomato Juice. Same spices as in Bloody Mary (see opposite). Shake well and strain.

Bloody Mary

In shaker or directly in large tumbler: ice, 6 dashes of Worcester Sauce, 3 dashes of Tabasco, pinch of salt, pinch of pepper, juice of ½ lemon, 2 ounces of Vodka, fill remainder of glass with top quality Tomato Juice, and above all no celery salt. *(Recipe: Pete Petiot, Bartender at Harry's Bar, Paris, 1921; he later became Captain of Bars at the St Regis Hotel, New York.)*

Blue Blazer

Take two silver or pewter mugs; in one melt one lump of sugar in boiling water that half fills one mug, in the other pour half-way some pre-warmed Scotch and ignite it. When the Whisky blazes brilliantly, pour it into the other mug rapidly, then pour the mixture back and forth deftly and with equal speed about six or seven times, thus producing a blaze of light. Bourbon, Rye or Rum may be used.

Blue Lagoon Cocktail

⅓ Blue Curaçao, ⅓ Vodka, ⅓ Lemon Juice. Shake and strain in bowl where an island of crushed and packed ice has been placed. Serve with straws piercing slice of lemon and orange; add a few cherries. *(Recipe: Andy MacElhone, Harry's Bar, Paris, 1960.)*

Blue Mountain

⅓ Williamine, ⅓ Blue Curaçao, ⅓ Grapefruit Juice. Shake and strain in cocktail glass. *(Recipe: Guy, Bartender at Harry's Bar, Paris, 1981.)*

Blue Ribbon Cocktail

⅔ Gin, ⅙ White Crème de Menthe, ⅙ Cointreau. Add 6 drops of Breton cooking dye; when shaken together, this dye gives a nice blue colour.
(Recipe: Harry MacElhone at Ciro's Club, London, 1919.)

Blue Seven

⅓ Blue Curaçao, ⅔ Smirnoff Vodka. Shake and strain in champagne glass. Fill with Champagne.
(Recipe: Marck, Bartender at Harry's Bar, Paris, 1977.)

Boca Beach

⅓ Vodka, ⅓ White Crème de Cacao, ⅙ fresh cream, ⅙ Coconut Cream. Shake and strain.
(Recipe: Harry's Bar, Munich.)

Boris Becker

In large tumbler: ice, juice of ½ lemon, 1 ounce of Bols Kiwi Wonder, 2 ounces of Smirnoff Vodka. Fill up with Pineapple Juice. Decorate glass with peeled Lychee as tennis ball.
(Recipe: Harry's Bar, Munich, 1985, for Davis Cup.)

Bosom Caresser

1 yolk of egg, 1 teaspoonful of Grenadine, ⅙ Cointreau, ⅙ Cognac, ⅓ Madeira. Shake and strain.

Boston

Prepare in rock glass: chopped ½ Lemon, ½ Orange, 2 teaspoons Brown Sugar. Add ⅞ Dark Rum, ⅛ Vodka, ⅞ Lemon Squash, ⅞ Orange Juice, ⅛ Lemon Juice. Fill with crushed ice, float 1 dash Calvados atop.
(Recipe: Andreas Lanninger, Berlin, 1993.)

Brandy Cocktail

2 ounces of Cognac, 2 dashes of Orange Curaçao, 2 dashes of Angostura. Stir and strain.

Brandy Crustas

Take a small tumbler, moisten the rim with lemon, dip rim of glass into castor sugar, which action gives the glass a frosted appearance. Cut the rind of ½ lemon the same way as you would an apple, then fit into your prepared glass. Then pour into your shaker 1 teaspoonful of sugar, 3 dashes of Maraschino, 3 dashes of Angostura, juice of ¼ lemon, 2 ounces of Cognac. Shake well, pour into your glass and add fruit.

Brandy Daisy

⅔ Cognac, ⅙ Grenadine, juice of ½ lemon. Shake well, pour in small tumbler, add cherry and fruit of the season and a squirt of Soda Water.

Brandy Fix

Pour in small tumbler: 1 teaspoonful of sugar, a little water to melt the sugar, juice of ½ lemon, ⅓ Cherry Brandy, ⅔ Cognac. Fill with shaved ice, stir slowly.

Brandy Flip

1 yolk of egg, 1 teaspoonful of sugar, 2 ounces of Cognac. Shake and strain in small tumbler and grate a nutmeg on top.

Brandy Julep

Same as Mint Julep (see p. 69).

Brandy Punch

In large tumbler: fill with shaved ice, 1 teaspoonful of Pineapple Syrup, juice of ¼ lemon, a few drops of Lime Juice, 2 ounces of Cognac, a squirt of Soda. Stir well, decorate with fruit and float a little 150 Proof Rum on top.

Brandy Shamparelle

¼ Red Curaçao, ¼ Yellow Chartreuse, ¼ Anisette, ¼ Cognac. Stir well and strain.

Brandy Smash

Muddle in shaker: 1 lump of sugar, a few drops of water, a few sprigs of mint, add 2 ounces of Cognac, ice. Shake well, strain in small tumbler filled with shaved ice. Decorate with sugar-coated sprig of mint.

Brandy Sour

1 teaspoonful of sugar, juice of a lemon, 2 ounces of Cognac. Shake and strain into wine glass, add cherry.

Brazil Cocktail

½ Dry Martini Vermouth, ½ Sherry, 3 dashes of Anis, 3 dashes of Angostura. Stir and strain.

Broken Spur Cocktail

1 yolk of egg, ⅙ Gin, ⅙ Sweet Vermouth, ⅔ White Port, 1 dash of Anisette. Shake and strain.

Bronx Cocktail

⅓ Gin, ⅓ Sweet Vermouth, juice of an orange. Shake and strain.

Brooklyn Cocktail

1 dash of American Picon, 1 dash of Maraschino, ⅔ Rye Whiskey, ⅓ Dry Vermouth. Stir and strain.

Brown Jug Cocktail

½ Kahlua, ½ Scotch Whisky. Stir and strain.

Bruno's Torpedo

Pack small tumbler with shaved ice, pour 2 ounces of Southern Comfort, twist orange peel, add more shaved ice, float 151 Proof Malt Whisky. Serve with short straws.
(Recipe: J. Bruno, Pen and Pencil Restaurant, New York.)

Bull-Dog Cocktail

In tumbler: ice, juice of 1 orange, 2 ounces of Gin. Fill balance with Ginger Ale. Stir and serve with straws.

Bull Shot Cocktail

2 ounces of Vodka, 5 ounces of Beef Broth, pinch of salt, pinch of pepper, 3 dashes of Tabasco, 3 dashes of Worcester Sauce. Shake well and strain in small tumbler.

Bunny's Cocktail

⅓ Gin, ⅓ Rye Whiskey, ⅓ Anis. Stir and strain.

Café de Paris Cocktail

1 white of egg, 3 dashes of Anisette, 2 ounces of Gin, 1 teaspoonful of cream. Shake and strain.

Can-Can Cocktail

⅓ Dry Vermouth, ⅓ Absinthe, ⅓ Rye Whiskey. Stir and strain.
(Recipe: Wells M. Adams, New York.)

Cape Codder

In large tumbler: ice, 2 ounces of Smirnoff Vodka, juice of ½ lime. Fill with Loganberry Juice.
(Recipe: L. Cyr, Sandwich, Mass., 1985.)

Cape Town Cocktail

½ Cape Brandy, ½ Van der Hum, 3 dashes of Curaçao, 2 dashes of Angostura. Stir and strain.

Caresse Cocktail

⅙ Cherry Brandy, ⅙ Crème de Cacao, ⅔ Cognac, 1 yolk of egg. Shake and pour.

Caribbean Sunset

¼ Cachaça, ¼ Cognac ★★★, ¼ Banana Liqueur, ¼ Lemon Juice, 4 dashes simple syrup. Shake and strain.
(Recipe: Duncan MacElhone, Paris, 1986.)

Carrol Cocktail

⅓ Sweet Vermouth, ⅔ Cognac. Stir and serve in glass with pickled walnut.
(Recipe: Plaza Hotel, New York, 1911.)

Caruso Cocktail

⅓ Gin, ⅓ Dubonnet, ⅓ Dry Vermouth. Stir and serve.
(Recipe: Henry Wm. Thomas, Drivers Bar, Washington.)

Casino Cocktail

In champagne glass: 1 lump of sugar soaked in Anis, 1 lump of ice, fill glass with Champagne, float dash of Cognac on top, squeeze lemon peel.

Cecil Pick-Me-Up

1 yolk of egg, 2 ounces of Cognac, 1 teaspoonful of sugar. Shake well and strain in large glass, fill balance with Champagne.
(Recipe: Wm. Pollack, Cecil Bar, London, 1926.)

Champagne Cocktail

In wine glass: 1 lump of sugar saturated with Angostura, 5 dashes of Cognac, ice, fill up with Champagne, squeeze peel of lemon.

Champagne Julep

In large wine glass: 1 teaspoonful of sugar, sprig of mint, shaved ice. Muddle well, add Champagne slowly, stirring gently all the time, decorate with sugar-coated fresh mint, float a little Cognac on top.

Champagne Pick-Me-Up

½ Cognac, ½ Dry Vermouth, 1 teaspoonful of sugar. Shake well and strain in wine glass; fill up with Champagne.

Chancellor

In mixing glass: ½ Scotch Whisky, ¼ Port, ¼ Martini Dry Vermouth, 2 dashes of Angostura. Stir and strain into cocktail glass.

Chapala

In shaker: ice, ½ Tequila, ¼ Orange Juice, ¼ Lemon Juice. Add few drops of Orange Flower Water, shake and strain.

Chapultepec

⅔ Gin, ⅓ White Crème de Cacao. Shake well and strain into small tumbler, on the rocks, decorate with mint-leaf.
(Recipe: E. Aldrete, Beverly Hills Hotel, Beverly Hills, Cal.)

Cherry Bomb Cocktail

⅔ 101 Proof Bourbon, ⅓ Cherry Brandy, 1 white of egg. Shake well and strain, add cherry.

ChinChina

³⁄₁₀ China Martini, ³⁄₁₀ Wild Strawberry Liqueur, ⁴⁄₁₀ Vodka. Stir and strain, finish with orange twist.
(Recipe: Thierry Delamare, Paris, 1988.)

Chinese Cocktail

3 dashes each of Angostura, Maraschino, Curaçao, Grenadine, 2 ounces of Rum from Jamaica. Shake, strain.

Christina

⅓ Gin, ⅓ Cherry Heering, ⅓ Orange Juice.
Shake and strain in cocktail glass, decorate with
maraschino cherry.
(Recipe: Mark, Harry's Bar, Paris, 1984.)

Cliftonian Cocktail

⅛ Caloric Punch, ⅜ Grand Marnier, ⅜ Gin, ⅛
Orange Juice. Shake and strain.

Clover Club Cocktail

1 white of egg, juice of small lime, 1 teaspoonful
of Grenadine, ⅓ Gin, ⅙ Sweet Vermouth. Shake
and strain.

Coronation Cocktail

2 dashes of Maraschino, 3 dashes of Orange Bit-
ters, ⅔ Dry Vermouth, ⅓ Sherry. Stir and strain.
*(Recipe: Joseph Rose, Murray Bros' Café,
Newark, N.J., 1903.)*

Coronation 1937 Cocktail

⅓ Scotch Whisky, ⅓ Grapefruit Juice, ⅙ Lemon
Juice, ⅙ Grenadine, 2 dashes of Angostura, 1
dash of Peach Bitters. Shake and strain in cocktail glass with small chunk of pineapple.
*(Recipe: Harry MacElhone, Harry's Bar, Paris,
1937.)*

Corpse Reviver

⅓ Sweet Vermouth, ⅓ Calvados, ⅓ Cognac.
Shake and strain.

Coucou Cumber

2 ounces of Smirnoff Vodka, sugar to taste, 4 to 5 drops of Pernod, shake well and strain in hollowed-out half cucumber.

Crazy Crossing Cocktail

½ Gin, ¼ Sweet Vermouth, ¼ Dubonnet, 1 dash of Maraschino. Stir and strain.

Cyberdry

⅘ Pisco, ⅕ Melon Liqueur, 1 dash Angostura, 1 dash Noilly Prat. Stir and strain.
(Recipe: Gilles Chauvain, Paris, 1996.)

Daiquiri Cocktail

¾ White Rum, ¼ Lime Juice (fresh), sugar. Shake well and strain.

Daisy

In small tumbler: ice, 2 ounces of Tequila, juice of ½ lemon, dash of Grenadine. Fill with Soda, stir and serve.

Dandy Cocktail

½ Rye Whiskey, ½ Dubonnet, 1 dash of Angostura, 3 dashes of Cointreau. Shake and strain, add lemon and orange peel.

Dark Rose

²⁄₁₀ Amaretto, ²⁄₁₀ Coffee Liqueur, ⁶⁄₁₀ Suze. Stir and strain.
(Recipe: Jean-Marc Vettesi, Paris, 1993.)

D'Artagnan

In shaker: ice, ⅓ Armagnac, ⅓ Cointreau, ⅓ Orange Juice. Shake and strain in large champagne glass, fill up with Champagne.
(Recipe: Andy MacElhone, Harry's Bar, Paris, 1985.)

Derby Cocktail

2 dashes of Peach Bitters, 1 sprig of mint, 2 ounces of Gin. Stir and strain in glass with olive.
(Recipe: E.G. de Gastreaux, Canal and Vine St., Cincinnati, 1903.)

Devil's Tail

Ice, ⅔ Light Rum, ⅓ Vodka, juice of ¼ lime, dash of Grenadine, dash of Apricot Brandy. Shake well and strain in cocktail glass.

Diabolo Cocktail

⅔ Dubonnet, ⅓ Gin, 2 dashes of Orgeat Syrup. Stir and strain.
(Recipe: F. Newman, Paris, 1933.)

Diki-Diki Cocktail

⅔ Calvados, ⅙ Swedish Punsch, ⅙ Grapefruit Juice. Shake and strain.

Doctor Cocktail

⅓ Swedish Punsch, ⅓ Lemon Juice, ⅓ Orange Juice. Shake and strain.

Dolce Vita

¾ Amaretto, ¼ Triple Sec, equal parts Orange and Pineapple Juice, 1 dash Lemon Juice, 1 dash Cream. Shake well and strain.
(Recipe: Andreas Lanninger, Berlin, 1993.)

Dôme Cocktail

⅓ Dubonnet, ⅓ Gin, ⅓ Anisette, 3 dashes of Orgeat Syrup. Shake and strain.
(Recipe: Carey, Bartender of the Bar at the Café Dôme, Paris, 1935.)

Double Eagle

⅓ 101 Proof Bourbon Whiskey, ⅓ Southern Comfort, ⅓ Lemon Juice. Shake and strain.
(Recipe: Duncan MacElhone, Harry's Bar, Paris, 1978.)

Dragon Boat Cocktail

In shaker: ice, 2 drops Angostura, ⅔ Vodka, ⅓ Kiwi Liqueur (Kibowi), spoonful Coconut Cream. Fill up with Pineapple Juice, serve with ice in tall tumbler, decorate with Cherry.
(Recipe: Mr James Smith, Dragon Boat Bar, Hong Kong Hilton, April 1986.)

Dream Cocktail

⅓ Curaçao, ⅔ Cognac, 2 dashes of Anis. Stir and strain.

Dream of the Blue Turtles

³⁄₆ Vodka, ²⁄₆ Blue Curaçao, ²⁄₆ Coconut Cream, equal parts Pineapple, Mango and Orange Juice, 3 dashes Cream. Shake well and strain.
(Recipe: Bernd Schäfer, Freudenpark, Nürnberg, 1990.)

Dubonnet Cocktail

⅔ Dubonnet, ⅓ Gin. Stir and strain.

Dunlop Cocktail

⅓ Sherry, ⅔ Rum, 1 dash of Angostura. Stir and strain.

Eagle's Dream Cocktail

1 teaspoonful of sugar, 1 white of egg, ⅔ Gin, ⅓ Crème Yvette, ⅓ Lemon Juice. Shake and strain in glass with cherry.

East India Cocktail

1 teaspoonful of Pineapple Syrup and one of Curaçao, 2 dashes of Angostura, 2 ounces of Cognac. Stir and strain in glass with cherry.

Egg Nog

1 egg, 1 teaspoonful of sugar, 2 ounces of Rum or 1 ounce of Rum and 1 ounce of Cognac, cold milk. Shake well, strain into medium-sized tumbler. Grate some nutmeg on top.

Egg Nog Hot

In a bowl: sugar to taste, 1 egg. Beat well with whisk, adding boiling milk, pour into tankard where 1 ounce of Rum and 1 ounce of Cognac have been poured, grate some nutmeg on top.

El Diablo

In tall tumbler: 2 ounces of Tequila, juice of ½ lime, ½ ounce of Crème de Cassis. Fill up with ginger ale, stir, decorate with slice of lime.

Elk's Own Cocktail

White of egg, ⅓ Rye Whiskey, ⅓ Port, ⅓ Lemon Juice, sugar. Shake and strain, add slice of pineapple.

Emerald

4/10 Gin, 4/10 Blue Curaçao, 2/10 Lime Cordial. Stir and strain.
(Recipe: Duncan MacElhone, Paris, 1977.)

Emotional Rescue

1/3 Sloe Gin, 1/3 Gin, 1/3 Cherry Liqueur, 2 dashes of Grenadine. Stir and strain. Decorate with Maraschino Cherry.
(Recipe: Roger, Paris, 1979.)

Empire Punch

In large tumbler: 1 teaspoonful each of Maraschino, Curaçao, Benedictine, Cognac, small amount of Claret. Fill balance with Champagne, shaved ice and decorate with fruit in season.

Enzo Ferrari

3/10 Grappa, 2/10 Cherry Brandy, 2/10 Lemon Juice, 3/10 Orange Juice, 2 dashes Grenadine. Shake well and strain.
(Recipe: Bernd Schäfer, Freudenpark, Nürnberg, 1989.)

Eskie Cocktail

In old-fashioned glass: ice, 2 ounces of Bourbon Whiskey, 1 dash of Angostura, 1 teaspoonful each of Benedictine and Sweet Martini Vermouth. Add cherry, slice of orange and pineapple.

Fallen Angel

¾ Gin, ¼ Lemon Juice, 2 dashes of Green Crème de Menthe, 1 dash of Angostura. Shake and strain.

Fantasio Cocktail

⅓ Gin, ⅓ Cognac, ⅙ White Mint, ⅙ Maraschino. Shake and strain.

Favourite Cocktail

⅓ Gin, ⅓ Dry Vermouth, ⅓ Apricot Brandy, 1 dash Lemon Juice. Shake and strain.

Fish House Punch

In a large tumbler: ice, 2 ounces of Bourbon Whiskey, juice of one lemon. Add Soda Water, float a little 150 Proof Rum on top, decorate with fruit in season, serve with straws.

Flying Elephant

⁴⁄₁₀ Vodka, ²⁄₁₀ Galliano, ³⁄₁₀ Pineapple Juice, ¹⁄₁₀ Coconut Milk, 4 dashes Cream. Shake well and strain.

Fog Horn Cocktail

⅔ Peach Brandy, ⅓ Dry Vermouth, 3 dashes of Grenadine. Shake and strain.

Four Flusher Cocktail

⅔ Bacardi, ⅙ Dry Vermouth, ⅙ Swedish Punsch, 2 dashes of Grenadine. Shake and strain.
(Recipe: Harry Craddock, Savoy Hotel Bar, London.)

Fox River Cocktail

In small tumbler: 1 lump of sugar saturated with Peach Bitters, 2 ounces of Bourbon Whiskey, 1 teaspoonful of Crème de Cacao, ice. Squeeze lemon peel on top.

Free and Easy Cocktail

In large tumbler: ice, 2 ounces of Gin. Fill with Coca Cola, add slice of lemon.
(Recipe: Ray Powers, Iroquois Ambulance Service, Paris, 1940.)

French '75

Shake 2 ounces of Gin, juice of a lemon, sugar, ice. Strain in large champagne glass and add Champagne; a teaspoonful of Anis may be added.
(Recipe: Harry's Bar, Paris, 1925.)

Frozen Fjord

$2/10$ Kümmel, $4/10$ White Aquavit, $4/10$ Cranberry Juice, 1 dash Lime Juice. Stir and strain over crushed ice in snifter.
(Recipe: Duncan MacElhone, Paris, 1990.)

Gentle Bull

In small tumbler: ice, 1 ounce of Tequila, 1 ounce of Kahlua. Stir and float double cream on top.

Gibson

⁹⁄₁₀ Gin, ¹⁄₁₀ Dry Vermouth. Stir and strain, add pearl onion.

Gilroy Cocktail

⅓ Gin, ⅓ Dry Vermouth, ⅙ Cherry Brandy, ⅙ Kirsch. Shake and strain.

Gimlet

⅔ Gin, ⅓ Lime Juice Cordial. Shake and strain.

Gin Daisy

Same as Brandy Daisy (see p. 37), but use Gin instead of Cognac.

Gin Fix

Same as Brandy Fix (see p. 37).

Gin Fizz

1 teaspoonful of sugar, juice of a lemon, 2 ounces of Gin. Shake well, add Soda Water, strain in medium-sized tumbler, decorate with cherry and slice of lemon.

Gin Julep

Prepared the same way as Mint Julep (see p. 69).

Gin Rickey

In small tumbler: ice, 2 ounces of Gin. Squeeze half a lime, and drop fruit in the glass.

Gin Sling

Juice of a lemon, 2 ounces of Gin, 1 teaspoonful of Grenadine, small amount of plain water. Shake and strain into medium-sized tumbler.

Gingersnap

⅔ Smirnoff Vodka, ⅓ Ginger Wine, ice. Shake well, pour into tumbler ice included, and add soda water.

Gloom Chaser Cocktail

⅙ Curaçao, ⅙ Grand Marnier, ⅙ Grenadine, ⅙ Lemon Juice, ⅓ Bacardi Rum. Shake and strain.

Golden Cadillac

⅓ Galliano, ⅓ White Crème de Cacao, ⅓ fresh cream. Shake well and strain.

Golden Dawn

¼ Gin, ¼ Calvados, ¼ Apricot Brandy, ¼ Orange Juice. Shake and strain, add a dash of Grenadine after cocktail is poured.

Golden Fizz

Similar to Gin Fizz (p. 53), yolk of fresh egg added.

Golden Gleam

⅓ Cognac, ⅓ Grand Marnier, ⅓ Orange Juice. Shake and strain.

Golden Heath

⅓ Drambuie, ⅓ Rum, ⅓ Sherry. Shake and strain.

Golden Slipper

In small tumbler: 1 ounce of Yellow Chartreuse, drop yolk of fresh egg, 1 ounce of Eau de Vie de Dantzig.
(Recipe: Harry Johnson, New Orleans.)

Grasshopper

⅓ White Crème de Cacao, ⅓ Green Crème de Menthe, ⅓ fresh cream. Shake well and strain.

Green Banana

²⁄₁₀ Pisang Ambon, ³⁄₁₀ White Rum, ⁴⁄₁₀ Banana Juice, ¹⁄₁₀ Coconut Milk, 4 dashes Cream. Shake well and strain.
(Recipe: Roger Gelly, Paris, 1984.)

Green Dragon

On the rocks, in a small tumbler: ½ Green Crème de Menthe, ½ Vodka.

Green Lady

⅔ Gin, ⅙ Green Chartreuse, ⅙ Yellow Chartreuse. Shake and strain, add lemon peel.
(Recipe: Georges Pesce, Fouquet's Bar, Paris.)

Grenadier Cocktail

1 dash of Jamaica Ginger, ⅓ Ginger Brandy, ⅔ Cognac, 1 teaspoonful of Gomme Syrup. Shake and strain.

Gringo Killer

⁴⁄₁₀ Mescal, ²⁄₁₀ Melon Liqueur, ⁴⁄₁₀ Pineapple Juice. In tumbler with powdered cinnamon stirred in.
(Recipe: Gilles Chauvain, Paris, 1996.)

Happy Youth Cocktail

In medium-sized tumbler: ice, juice of 1 orange, 2 ounces of Cherry Brandy. Fill balance with Champagne.
(Recipe: Charlie Soumille, Harry's Bar, Paris, 1938.)

Harricane®

$^2/_{10}$ Malt Whisky, $^3/_{10}$ Dry Sherry. In tumbler with ice. Finish with $^5/_{10}$ Ginger Ale.

Harry's Cocktail

$^2/_3$ Gin, $^1/_3$ Sweet Vermouth, 1 dash of Absinthe, 2 sprigs of mint. Shake well and strain, serve with a stuffed olive.
(Recipe: Harry MacElhone, Aix-les-Bains Casino Bar, 1910.)

Harry's Pick-Me-Up

2 dashes of Grenadine, juice of ½ lemon, 2 ounces of Cognac. Shake well and strain in medium-sized tumbler, fill balance with Champagne.
(Recipe: Harry MacElhone, Harry's Bar, Paris, 1925.)

Harvard Cocktail

½ Cognac, ½ Sweet Martini Vermouth, 2 dashes of Angostura, 1 dash of Gomme Syrup. Shake and strain.

Harvey Wallbanger

In tall tumbler: ice, 2 ounces of Vodka. Fill ¾ full with Orange Juice, float 1 ounce of Galliano on top.

Havowon Cocktail

⅓ Gin, ⅙ Dubonnet, ⅙ Loganberry Fruit Juice, ⅓ Dry Vermouth. Shake and strain.
(Recipe: Jock Melville, 500 Club, London, 1941.)

Holly

³⁄₁₀ Dark Rum, ¹⁄₁₀ Vanilla 'Bourbon' Liqueur, ⁴⁄₁₀ Pineapple Juice, ¹⁄₁₀ Lime Juice. Shake well and strain.
(Recipe: Jean-Marc Vettesi, Paris, 1995.)

Honeysuckle Cocktail

2 ounces of White Rum, ¼ ounce of liquid honey, juice of ½ lemon. Shake well and strain.

Horse's Neck

Peel the rind of a lemon, in one piece and in a spiral, place one end of the peel over the rim of a tall tumbler, allowing rest to curl inside, fill with ice, add 2 ounces of Cognac, fill balance with Ginger Ale. Either Rum or Whisky can be used instead.

Hot Buttered Rum

2 ounces of Dark Rum, sugar to taste, stick of Cinnamon, boiling water, small amount of butter. Stir and serve; extra butter can be served on a side plate.

Hurricane Cocktail

⅔ Gin, ⅓ Sherry. Stir and strain, add lemon peel.
(Recipe: Harry MacElhone, Café de Paris, London, 1941.)

IBF Pick-Me-Up

In large champagne glass: ice, 3 dashes of Fernet Branca, 3 dashes of Curaçao, 2 ounces of Cognac, fill remainder with Champagne. Stir and squeeze lemon peel on top.

Inca Cocktail

¼ Gin, ¼ Dry Vermouth, ¼ Sweet Martini Vermouth, ¼ Sherry, 1 dash of Orange Bitters, 1 dash of Orgeat Syrup. Stir and strain.

Incognito Cocktail

⅓ Cognac, ⅓ Dry Vermouth, ⅓ Apricot Brandy, 1 dash of Angostura. Shake and strain.

Ink Street Cocktail

⅓ Rye Whiskey, ⅓ Lemon Juice, ⅓ Orange Juice. Shake and strain.

Irish Coffee

In a warm Irish Coffee glass: sugar to taste, 2 ounces of Irish Whiskey. Fill nearly to brim of glass with strong black coffee, dilute sugar, then float up to brim Fresh Cream, with the help of the back of your bar-spoon.

Irish Fizz

2 ounces of Irish Whiskey, juice of ½ lemon, teaspoonful of Curaçao. Shake and strain into medium-sized tumbler, fill up with Soda, add lemon slice and green cherry.

Jack Rose Cocktail

2 ounces of Calvados, juice of a lemon, 4 dashes of Grenadine. Shake and strain.

James Bond Cocktail

In champagne glass: lump of sugar saturated with Angostura, ice, 2 ounces of Vodka, fill with Champagne, add lemon peel.
(Recipe: Andy MacElhone, Harry's Bar, Paris.)

Jersey Cocktail

In tumbler: ice, 3 dashes of Angostura, 1 ounce of Apple-jack. Fill with Cider, stir and serve.

John John Cocktail

4 dashes of Cherry Brandy, ⅔ Gin, ⅙ Dry Vermouth, ⅙ Poire William. Stir and strain, add a cherry.
(Recipe: Jean Doreau, Grand Hotel Bar, Paris.)

Journalist Cocktail

1 dash of Angostura, 2 dashes of Curaçao, 2 dashes of Lemon Juice, ⅙ Dry Vermouth, ⅙ Sweet Vermouth, ⅓ Gin. Stir and serve.

Kamikaze

⁶⁄₁₀ Vodka, ³⁄₁₀ Lime Cordial, ¹⁄₁₀ Lemon Juice, 1 dash Triple Sec. Shake and strain on crushed ice.

Kanzler Cocktail

Juice of ½ lemon. ⅔ Bourbon, ⅓ Cointreau. Shake, strain in champagne glass, fill with Champagne, decorate with thin slice of cucumber.
(Recipe: Harry's Bar, Munich, 1977.)

King Pin Cocktail

In large champagne glass: 2 ounces of Cognac, ice. Fill with Champagne, add orange peel.

Knickebein Cocktail

⅔ Cognac, ⅙ Maraschino, ⅙ Grenadine, 1 egg yolk. Shake well and strain in small tumbler.

Knickerbocker Cocktail

1 teaspoonful each of: Raspberry Syrup, Lemon Juice, Orange Juice, 2 dashes of Curaçao, ⅔ Rum. Shake and strain, add small chunk of pineapple.

Knock-out Cocktail

⅓ Gin, ⅓ Dry Vermouth, ⅓ Absinthe or Anis, 1 teaspoon of White Crème de Menthe. Shake and strain.
(Recipe invented for Gene Tunney, when he became Heavyweight Champion of the World.)

K2 Cocktail

⅓ Vodka, ⅓ Lemon Juice, ⅓ Vervaine du Velay (green). Shake and strain in glass filled with shaved ice.

(Recipe: Andy MacElhone, Harry's Bar, Paris, when the French mountaineering team set up a Harry's Bar at their base camp, on K2 in 1979.)

LAD Cocktail

Fill large brandy snifter full of shaved ice, 2 ounces of Cointreau, float Cognac on top.
(Recipe: Andy MacElhone, Harry's Bar, Paris, 1954.)

Lady Finger Cocktail

½ Gin, ¼ Kirsch, ¼ Cherry Brandy. Stir and strain.

Lasky Cocktail

⅓ Gin, ⅓ Swedish Punsch, ⅓ Grape Juice. Shake and strain.

Liberty

⅓ I.W. Harper Bourbon Whiskey, ⅓ Martini Dry Vermouth, ⅙ Lime Juice cordial, ⅙ Southern Mist. Shake and strain in cocktail glass. This cocktail was created at Harry's Bar Paris, by Duncan MacElhone, for the Franco-American Committee for the restoration of the Statue of Liberty, part of the sale price being given to the Committee until 4th July, 1986.

Light Breeze (alcohol free)

In a rock glass cut Lime in eight, cover with Brown Sugar and Lime Juice Cordial and crush to a pulp, add 2 dashes of Angostura and finish with Ginger Ale.
(Recipe: Peter Kallweit, MS Europa, 1990.)

Lillian Waldorf Cocktail

In small liquor glass pour very carefully ½ Maraschino, ½ Crème Yvette. Top with cream.

Locomotive Cocktail

1 teaspoonful of liquid honey, 1 teaspoonful of Curaçao, 1 yolk of egg, 1 small glass of Port Wine. Shake well and pour in medium-sized tumbler.

Lollipop

In tall tumbler: ice, 1 ounce of Blue Curaçao, 1 ounce of Banana Liqueur, juice of ½ a lemon. Fill up with Orange Juice, decorate with cherry. *(Recipe: François, Harry's Bar, Munich, 1983.)*

London Fog Cocktail

½ White Crème de Menthe, ½ Anisette, 1 dash of Angostura. Shake and strain.

Long Drive (alcohol free)

Orange Juice, 4 dashes Almond Syrup, 2 dashes Grenadine. Shake and strain. *(Recipe: Duncan MacElhone, Paris, 1987.)*

Love Cocktail

¾ Sloe Gin, 1 white of egg, 2 dashes of Lemon Juice, 2 dashes of Raspberry Syrup. Shake and strain.

Luigi Cocktail

1 Cointreau, 1 teaspoonful of Grenadine, ⅓ Tangerine Juice, ⅓ Gin, ⅓ Dry Vermouth. Shake, strain.

Magnolia Cocktail

1 teaspoonful of Curaçao and one of Gomme Syrup, 1 yolk of egg, 2 ounces of Cognac. Shake well and strain in medium-sized tumbler, fill balance with Champagne.

Mah Jongg Cocktail

⅙ Cointreau, ⅙ Bacardi, ⅔ Gin. Shake and strain.
(Recipe: Willie Dale, Romano's, London.)

Maiden's Blush Cocktail

⅔ Gin, ⅓ Anis, 1 teaspoonful of Grenadine. Shake and strain.

Mai-Tai Cocktail

In large tumbler: ice, 3 dashes of Orange Curaçao, 1 teaspoonful of Gomme Syrup, 1 ounce of White Rum, 1 ounce of Dark Rum, juice of ½ lemon and ½ lime. Stir well and garnish with fruit.

Makka Cocktail

In tumbler: ¼ Campari, ¼ Sweet Vermouth, ¼ Dry Vermouth, ¼ Gin, ice, slice of lemon. Top up with Soda Water.

Mambo-Jambo Cocktail

¼ Bourbon, ¼ Sweet Vermouth, ¼ Peach Brandy, ⅛ Pimm's No 1, ⅛ Lime Juice. Shake and strain.
(Recipe: Mike Cordova, The Brown Derby, Los Angeles.)

Manhattan Cocktail

Ice, ¾ Rye Whiskey, ¼ Sweet Vermouth, 2 dashes of Angostura. Stir and serve with cherry; for a dry cocktail use Dry Vermouth.

Margharita Cocktail

Ice, ⅓ Tequila, ⅓ Cointreau, ⅓ Lemon Juice. Shake well and serve in glass whose rim has been salt-coated.

Marmalade Cocktail

2 teaspoonfuls of Marmalade, juice of 1 lemon, 2 ounces of Gin, ice. Shake well and strain.

Martini Cocktail

The present-day taste is for a drier and drier Martini, so ⁹⁄₁₀ gin, ¹⁄₁₀ Dry Vermouth, or better still: Wash your ice in Dry Vermouth, then use ¹⁰⁄₁₀ Gin. Stir and serve.

Mary Pickford Cocktail

½ Light Rum, ½ unsweetened Pineapple Juice, 1 dash of Grenadine. Shake and strain.

Mayfair Cocktail

½ Gin, ½ Orange Juice, 3 dashes of Apricot Syrup, 1 dash of Clove Syrup. Shake and strain.

McClelland Cocktail

⅔ Sloe Gin, ⅓ Curaçao, ice, 1 dash of Orange Bitters. Stir and strain.

Melba Cocktail

½ Swedish Punsch, ½ Light Rum, 2 dashes of Grenadine, 2 dashes of Anis, ice. Shake and strain.

Metal Hurlant

In large tumbler: ice, 3 dashes Angostura, 2 ounces of Mescal, juice of ½ orange; fill up with Ginger Ale, slice of orange.
(Recipe: Andy MacElhone, Harry's Bar, Paris, 1985.)

Mighty Fine Cocktail

Ice, ⅓ Rye Whiskey, ⅓ American Picon, ⅓ Orange Juice, 2 dashes of Orange Bitters. Shake and strain.

Mile High Cocktail

In wide tumbler, for stability: 1 dash of Angostura, ⅓ Orange Juice, ⅔ Cognac. Fill up with Champagne, the plane will provide the shaking.
(Recipe: G.S., Sri Lanka, 1979.)

Millionaire Cocktail

Ice, 1 white of egg, 2 ounces of Rye Whiskey, 2 dashes of Orange Curaçao, 4 dashes of Grenadine. Shake.
(Recipe: Ritz Hotel Bar. London.)

Mint Julep

In tall tumbler: 8 or 10 leaves of mint, spoonful of sugar, a little plain water. Muddle the mint till the sugar has melted, pack half of the glass with shaved ice, pour 1 ounce of Bourbon Whiskey. Stir, add more shaved ice to top of tumbler. Stir, pour another ounce of Bourbon. Stir, float a small amount of 101 Proof Bourbon, decorate with sugar-coated sprig of mint, serve with straws.

Mississippi Mule Cocktail

Ice, ⅔ Gin, ⅙ Cassis, ⅙ Lemon Juice. Shake and strain.

Mistletoe Punch

In a tankard: half-fill with boiling water over a soup-spoon thick Honey. ⅓ Tawny Port, ⅓ Cognac ★★★, ⅓ Dark Rum. Decorate with a peeled lychee.
(Recipe: Andy MacElhone, Montreux, 1986.)

Moll Cocktail

⅓ Gin, ⅓ Sloe Gin, ⅓ Dry Vermouth, 1 dash of Orange Bitters. Shake and strain.

Monkey's Gland Cocktail

1 dash of Anis, 2 dashes of Grenadine, ½ Orange Juice, ½ Gin. Shake and strain.
(Recipe: Harry MacElhone, Harry's Bar, Paris, during Dr Voronoff's experiments.)

Montana Cocktail

2 dashes of Anis, 3 dashes of Orange Bitters, ½ Dry Vermouth, ½ Sloe Gin. Stir, serve.

Monte Carlo Imperial

½ Gin, ¼ Lemon Juice, ¼ White Crème de Menthe. Shake well, strain in large champagne glass and fill up with Champagne.

Morning Glory Fizz

1 white of egg, 1 teaspoonful of sugar, juice of one lemon, 1 teaspoonful of Anis, 1 ounce of Rye Whiskey. Shake well, add Soda Water and serve in medium-sized tumbler.
(Recipe: Harry Johnson, New Orleans.)

Moscow Mule Cocktail

In large tankard: ice, juice of one lime, 2 ounces of Vodka. Fill up with Ginger Ale, decorate with sprig of mint.
(Recipe by Jack Morgan, Cock 'n' Bull Restaurant, Los Angeles.)

Moulin Rouge Cocktail

½ Orange Gin, ½ Apricot Brandy, 2 dashes of Grenadine. Stir and serve.

Mountain Cocktail

1 white of egg, ⅙ Lemon Syrup, ⅙ Dry Vermouth, ⅓ Rye Whiskey, 3 dashes of Orange Bitters. Shake well and strain.

Negroni Cocktail

In small tumbler: ice, 3 dashes of Angostura, ⅓ Campari, ⅓ Sweet Vermouth, ⅓ Gin. Top off with a little Soda Water, slice of orange.
(Recipe: Hotel Baglioni, Florence, 1920.)

Nelson's Blood

In shaker: ice, ⅓ Pusser's Rum, ⅓ Apple Juice, ⅙ Cranberry Juice, ⅙ Lemon Juice. Shake and strain in cocktail glass, add cherry.
(Recipe: Harry's Bar, Munich, 1986.)

New Orleans Gin Fizz

1 white of egg, 1 teaspoonful of sugar, 4 dashes of Fleur d'Oranger, 2 ounces of Gin, juice of one lemon, equivalent of ½ wine glass of cream. Shake well, add Soda Water and strain in medium-sized tumbler.

Nice Pear

⁷⁄₁₀ White young Armagnac, ²⁄₁₀ Pear Liqueur, ¹⁄₁₀ Lemon Juice. Stir and strain.
(Recipe: Patrick Foynard, Paris, 1989.)

Night-Cap Cocktail

1 yolk of egg, ⅓ Anisette, ⅓ Curaçao, ⅓ Cognac. Shake well and strain in small tumbler.

Nineteenth Hole Cocktail

⅓ Rye Whiskey, ⅓ Sweet Vermouth, ⅓ Sherry. Stir and serve.

Nineteen-Twenty Cocktail

1 dash of Anis, ⅙ Kirschwasser, ⅙ Gin, ⅔ Dry Vermouth, 1 teaspoonful of Groseille Syrup. Shake well and strain.

Normandie

⁵⁄₁₀ Calvados HA, ²⁄₁₀ Triple Sec, ²⁄₁₀ Lime Juice, ¹⁄₁₀ Grenadine, 1 Egg White. Shake well and strain.
(Recipe: Peter Kallweit, QE2, 1994.)

Old-fashioned Cocktail

In small tumbler: crush in a little plain water a lump of sugar saturated with Angostura, add ice, 2 ounces of Bourbon Whiskey, lemon peel. Stir and serve.

Old Pal Cocktail

⅓ Canadian Whiskey, ⅓ Dry Vermouth, ⅓ Campari. Stir and serve.
(Recipe: Sparrow Robinson, Sporting Editor, New York Herald Tribune, Paris, 1929.)

Old Potato Cocktail

⅔ Irish Whiskey, ⅙ Dry Vermouth, ⅙ Calvados. Shake and serve.

Old Trib Cocktail

⅙ White Rum, ⅙ Cointreau, ⅔ Dry Vermouth, 1 dash of Pernod.
(Recipe: Lee Dickson, Paris, 1926.)

Olympic Cocktail

⅓ Cognac, ⅓ Curaçao, ⅓ Orange Juice. Shake well and serve.
(Recipe: Frank Meyer, Ritz Hotel Bar, Paris.)

Once Over Cocktail

⅓ Pernod, ⅓ American Picon, ⅙ Suze, ⅙ Grenadine. Shake well and strain.

Opera Cocktail

⅔ Gin, ⅙ Dubonnet, ⅙ Liqueur of Mandarine. Shake well and strain.

Orange Blossom

Juice of 1 orange, 2 ounces of Gin. Shake well and serve in small tumbler.

Ostende Fizz

½ Cassis, ½ Kirschwasser. Shake well, add Soda Water, serve in medium-sized tumbler.

Paradise Cocktail

⅓ Gin, ⅓ Apricot Brandy, ⅓ Orange Juice. Shake and strain.

Parisian Cocktail

⅓ Gin, ⅓ Dry Vermouth, ⅓ Crème de Cassis. Stir and serve.

Perfect Cocktail

⅓ Gin, ⅓ Dry Vermouth, ⅓ Sweet Vermouth. Stir and serve.

Peroquet Cocktail

In tall tumbler: 1 teaspoonful of Crème de Menthe, 2 ounces of Pernod. Add water to taste.

Petrifier Cocktail

In very large tankard: ice, 2 dashes of Angostura, 1 teaspoonful of Grenadine, 1 ounce each of Vodka, Cognac, Gin, White Rum, Grand Marnier, Cointreau. Top with Ginger Ale, float spoonful of Calvados on top, decorate with slices of lemon and orange.
(Recipe: Andy MacElhone, Harry's Bar, Paris, 1964.)

Pina Colada Cocktail

2 ounces of Jamaica Rum, ⅔ Pineapple Juice, ⅓ Coconut Cream. Shake well and pour in large tumbler, with ice, and decorate with fruit.

Ping-Pong Cocktail

1 teaspoonful of Lemon Juice, ½ Sloe Gin, ½ Crème Yvette. Shake and strain, add cherry.
(Recipe: James Bennet, Broken Heart Café, St Louis, 1903.)

Pink Gin Cocktail

Coat the inside of a wine glass with 4 or 5 dashes of Angostura, then pour 2 ounces of Gin, add water to taste. If lump of ice is added, this drink becomes a Coaster Cocktail.

Pink Lady Cocktail

1 white of egg, 2 ounces of Gin, 1 tablespoonful of Grenadine. Shake well and strain.

Pink Rose Cocktail

1 white of egg, 3 dashes of Grenadine, 1 tablespoonful of Lemon Juice and one of fresh cream, 2 ounces of Gin. Shake well and strain in small tumbler.

Planter's Punch

In large tumbler: ice, juice of 1 orange and 1 lemon, 1 dash of Grenadine, 1 ounce of White Rum, 1 ounce of Dark Rum. Stir, decorate with fruit.

Polo Cocktail

⅓ Gin, ⅓ Orange Juice, ⅓ Grapefruit Juice. Shake and serve.

Prairie Oyster Cocktail

In small tumbler: drop without breaking 1 yolk of egg, 2 spoonfuls of Worcester Sauce, 2 dashes of Tabasco, pinch of salt, pinch of pepper, 1 teaspoonful of malt vinegar.

President Cocktail

⅓ White Rum, ⅓ Curaçao, ⅓ Dry Martini Vermouth, 1 dash of Grenadine. Shake and strain.

Pretty Woman

²⁄₁₀ Peach Cordial, ⁴⁄₁₀ Cream, ¹⁄₁₀ Coconut Milk, ³⁄₁₀ Pineapple Juice, 1 dash Grenadine. Shake well and strain.
(Recipe: Andreas Gorgi, Berlin, 1990.)

Prince Charlie Cocktail

⅓ Curaçao, ⅓ Cognac, ⅓ Lemon Juice. Shake well and strain.

Prince of Wales Cocktail

⅓ Curaçao, ⅔ Cognac, 1 dash of Angostura, drop of lemon juice. Shake, strain into tankard and fill with Champagne.
(Recipe: Jack Van Land, Harry's Bar, Le Touquet, 1936.)

Princess Mary Cocktail

⅓ Gin, ⅓ White Crème de Cacao, ⅓ fresh cream. Shake well and strain.
(Recipe: London, Feb. 1922.)

Princeton Cocktail

2 dashes of Orange Bitters, 1 teaspoonful of Port Wine, 2 ounces of Gin. Shake well and strain, squeeze lemon peel on top.

Pussyfoot Cocktail

1 yolk of egg, 1 teaspoonful of Grenadine, juice of 1 lemon and 1 orange. Shake well and serve in tall glass with ice.

Quaker's Cocktail

⅓ Cognac, ⅓ Rum, ⅙ Raspberry Syrup. Shake well and strain.

Quarter-Deck Cocktail

1 teaspoonful of Cointreau, ⅓ American Picon, ⅔ Dubonnet. Shake well and strain.
(Recipe: Wilson, Dingo Bar, Paris, 1929.)

Queen Mary Cocktail

⅙ Grand Marnier, ⅙ Cointreau, ⅙ Dry Vermouth, ⅙ Lemon Juice, ⅙ Gin. Shake and strain.
(Recipe of 1936 to celebrate winning of the Blue Ribbon by SS Queen Mary.*)*

Queen's Cocktail

In shaker: place 2 slices of pineapple, muddle them, add ice, ⅓ Sweet Vermouth, ⅓ Dry Vermouth, ⅓ Gin. Shake well and pour in small tumbler.

Quill Cocktail

⅓ Campari, ⅓ Sweet Vermouth, ⅓ Gin, 1 dash of Anis. Stir and serve.
(Recipe: Frank C. Payne, New York.)

Raffles Bar Gin Sling

Juice of ½ lime, 2 dashes of Angostura, ⅓ Cherry Brandy, ⅔ Gin. Shake well and strain.

Rangoon Pimm's Cup

In Pimm's glass: 2 ounces of Pimm's, ice. Garnish with fruit, fill with Tonic Water, float a spoonful of Gin on top.

Reform Cocktail

1 dash of Orange Bitters, ⅓ Dry Martini Vermouth, ⅔ Sherry. Stir and strain.

Relax Cocktail

⅓ Chestnut Liqueur, ⅓ Cointreau, ⅓ Cream. Shake well and strain.
(Recipe: Philippe Recher, Paris, 1994.)

Reyno Cocktail

In tall glass: ice, ⅔ Vodka, ⅓ Crème de Menthe. Fill up with Tonic Water, decorate with sprig of fresh mint.
(Recipe: Harry's Bar, Munich, 1976.)

Rob Roy Cocktail

1 dash of Angostura, ⅔ Scotch Whisky, ⅓ Sweet Vermouth. Stir and strain, serve with cherry.

Rock and Rye Cocktail

In small tumbler: 1 teaspoonful of Rock Candy Syrup, 2 ounces of Rye Whiskey, juice of ½ lemon. Stir together, squeeze lemon peel on top.

Rose Cocktail

⅙ Kirschwasser, ⅙ Syrup of Groseille, ⅔ Dry Vermouth. Stir and serve with a cherry.
(Recipe: Johnny, Chatham Hotel Bar, Paris, 1919.)

Nowadays this cocktail is usually made as follows: ¼ Gin, ¼ Dry Vermouth, ¼ Kirschwasser, ¼ Cherry Brandy. Stir and serve with cherry.

Royal Cocktail

⅓ Gin, ⅓ Dry Vermouth, ⅓ Cherry Brandy, 1 dash of Maraschino. Shake and strain, serve with cherry.
(Recipe: Otis MacKinney, Hotel Royal, Nice, 1908.)

Royal Clover Club Cocktail

Juice of ½ lemon, 1 teaspoonful of Grenadine, 1 yolk of egg, 2 ounces of Gin. Shake well and strain in medium-sized tumbler. If Soda Water is added, it then becomes a Royal Fizz Cocktail.

Royal Mail Cocktail

¼ Orange Juice, ¼ Lemon Juice, ¼ Sloe Gin, ¼ Van der Hum, 1 dash of Anis. Shake and strain.

Royal Romance Cocktail

½ Gin, ¼ Grand Marnier, ¼ Passion Fruit, 1 dash of Grenadine. Shake and strain.

Royal Smile Cocktail

Juice of 1 lime, 3 dashes of Grenadine, ⅔ Calvados, ⅓ Gin. Shake and strain.

Ruby Fizz

1 teaspoonful of sugar, 1 whole fresh egg, 2 ounces of Gin. Shake well and pour in medium-sized tumbler, complete with Ginger Ale.
(Recipe: Wm. Yarrow of McDonagh Bros., Market St, San Francisco.)

Rum Boogie

1 dash each of Gomme Syrup, Curaçao, Anis, juice of 1 orange and 1 lemon, 1 ounce each of Light Rum, Cognac, Demerara Rum. Shake well and pour with the ice into very tall tumbler.

Rum Collins

Same as Tom Collins (see p. 91), but with Dark or Light Rum, according to taste.

Russell House Cocktail

2 dashes of Orange Bitters, 2 dashes of Rock Syrup, 3 dashes of Blackberry Brandy, 2 ounces of Rye Whiskey. Shake and strain.
(Recipe: Ed. V. Orsinger, Hotel Columbus, Harrisburg, Pa.)

Safe Speed (alcohol free)

⅓ Grapefruit Juice, ⅓ Lemon Juice, ⅓ Pineapple Juice, 2 dashes Grenadine, 1 dash Passion Fruit Liqueur or Juice, 1 Egg White. Shake well and strain.
(Recipe: Duncan MacElhone, Paris, 1989.)

Saratoga Cocktail

1 teaspoonful of Pineapple Syrup, 2 dashes of Orange Bitters, 2 dashes of Maraschino, 2 ounces of Cognac. Shake well and strain in large wine glass, add 1 strawberry, and fill up with Champagne.

Sazerac Cocktail

Coat inside of old-fashioned glass with 4 dashes of Anis, crush 1 lump of sugar saturated with Angostura, fill with cracked ice, complete with 2 ounces of Bourbon Whiskey.

Scoff-Law Cocktail

1 dash of Orange Bitters, ⅓ Canadian Whiskey, ⅓ Dry Vermouth, ⅙ Lemon Juice, ⅙ Grenadine. Shake and strain.
(Recipe: Chicago Tribune, 27 January, 1924: Hardly has Boston added to the gaiety of nations by adding to Webster's Dictionary the opprobrious term of 'scoff-law', when Jock, the genial bartender of Harry's Bar in Paris, yesterday invented the Scoff-Law Cocktail, and it has already become exceedingly popular among American prohibition dodgers.)

Scorpion

In tumbler: ice, 1 ounce of Dark Rum, 1 ounce of Light Rum. Fill with Maracuya Juice.

Screwdriver

In tall tumbler: ice, 2 ounces of Vodka. Fill up with Orange Juice, garnish with orange slice.

Sea Breeze

4/10 Vodka, 3/10 Cranberry Juice, 3/10 Grapefruit Juice. Shake well and strain.

'75 Cocktail

1 teaspoonful of Absinthe, 2/3 Calvados, 1/3 Gin. Shake and strain.
(Recipe: This is the original 1915 recipe of the French '75 Cocktail.)

Shameless

4/10 Pisco, 1/10 Maraschino, 3/10 Lemon Juice, 2/10 Grapefruit Juice, 1 Egg White. Shake well and strain.
(Recipe: Jean-Marc Vettesi, Paris, 1993.)

Shandy Gaff

Equal parts Ginger Ale and Pale Ale.

Short Fuse

In large tumbler: 2 ounces of 101 Proof Tequila, ½ ounce of Apricot Brandy, 2 teaspoonfuls of Maraschino-cherry juice, ¾ ounce of Lime Juice, 3 ounces of Grapefruit Juice. Decorate with cherry and ½ slice orange.
(Recipe: E. Greenberg, New York.)

Short Life Cocktail

⅓ Vodka, ⅓ Calvados, ⅓ Pernod. Shake and strain.

Side-Car Cocktail

⅓ Cointreau, ⅓ Cognac, ⅓ Lemon Juice. Shake and strain.
(Recipe: Harry MacElhone, Harry's Bar, Paris, 1931.)

Silver Cocktail

1 white of egg, 2 dashes each of Orgeat Syrup, Maraschino, Orange Bitters, ⅓ Dry Vermouth, ⅔ Gin. Stir and serve.
(Recipe: Pat O'Brien, Knickerbocker Hotel, New York.)

Silver Streak Cocktail

½ Kümmel, ½ Gin. Shake well and strain.

Singapore Gin Sling

Juice of 1 lime or lemon, ¼ Cherry Brandy, ¾ Gin. Shake well, add Soda Water, pour in tall tumbler containing ice, slice of lemon and cherry.

Sir Walter Cocktail

4 dashes each of Grenadine, Curaçao, Lemon Juice, ½ Cognac, ½ Rum. Shake well and strain.

Six Cylinder Cocktail

⅙ Cherry Brandy, ⅙ Gin, ⅙ Campari, ⅙ Dubonnet, ⅙ Dry Vermouth, ⅙ Sweet Vermouth.

Skye Boat Cocktail

In medium-sized tumbler: fill with cracked ice, ⅓ Orange Juice, ⅓ Drambuie, ⅓ Scotch Whisky. Stir, float on top extra large peel of orange, with lump of sugar, impregnated with 101 Proof Malt Whisky, to which you set fire.
(Recipe: Andy MacElhone, Harry's Bar, Paris, 1965.)

Snowball Cocktail

⅓ Gin, ⅓ White Crème de Menthe, ⅙ Anisette, ⅙ fresh cream. Shake well and strain.

South of the Border

⅗ Tequila, ⅖ Coffee Liqueur, Juice of ½ Lime. Stir and stir.

Southern Beauty Cocktail

1 teaspoonful of Lemon Syrup, juice of 1 lime, 2 ounces of Cognac. Shake and pour in tumbler, complete with Soda Water.

Southern Belle

³⁄₁₀ Peach Liqueur, ²⁄₁₀ Bourbon, ⁵⁄₁₀ Peach Juice, 1 dash Angostura. Shake well and strain. Top off with Champagne.
(Recipe: Duncan MacElhone, Paris, 1988.)

Spirit of St Louis Cocktail

2 ounces of Gin, 1 white of egg, 1 teaspoonful of Grenadine, 2 drops of Fleur D'Oranger. Shake well and strain in medium-sized tumbler.
(Recipe: Harry's Bar, Paris, 21 May, 1927, in honour of C. Lindbergh Flight.)

Spitfire Cocktail

⅓ Sherry, ⅓ Scotch, ⅓ Lime Juice Cordial. Shake and strain.
(Recipe: Harry MacElhone, Café de Paris, London, 1941.)

Star Cocktail

1 teaspoonful each of Grapefruit Juice, Dry Vermouth, Sweet Vermouth, ½ Gin, ½ Calvados. Shake well and strain.
(Recipe: Plaza Hotel, New York, 1911.)

Stinger Cocktail

½ Cognac, ½ White Crème de Menthe. Shake well and strain.

Stone Fence Cocktail

In tumbler: ice, 2 ounces of Rye Whiskey. Fill balance with Cider.

Suffering Bar Steward

In tall tumbler: ice, 2 ounces of Cognac, small glass of Dry Sherry. Complete with Ginger Ale, garnish with sprig of fresh mint.
(Recipe: Shepheard Hotel, Cairo. It quickly became known as Suffering Bastard Cocktail, and a great favourite with the 'Desert Rats' from 1941 to 1943.)

Swimming-Pool Cocktail

1 ounce of White Rum, ½ ounce each of Vodka, Blue Curaçao, Coconut Cream, fresh cream, 4 ounces of Pineapple Juice. Shake well and strain in very large tumbler, or better still in oversized Brandy snifter, filled with ice, and decorate with pineapple chunks and cherries.
(Recipe: Harry's Bar, Munich, 1980.)

Swisse Cocktail

1 white of egg, 1 teaspoonful of Anisette, 2 ounces of Anis. Shake well and strain in small tumbler, add dash of Soda Water on top.

Taipan Cocktail

In shaker: ice, ⅔ Vodka, ⅓ Orange Juice, splash of fresh cream and Banana Liqueur (Pisang Ambon) in medium-sized tumbler.
(Recipe: Mr Andreas Bossard, Dragon Boat Bar, Hong Kong Hilton, 29 April, 1986.)

Tango Cocktail

⅙ Curaçao, ⅙ Orange Juice, ⅓ Sweet Vermouth, ⅓ Gin. Shake and serve with orange peel.

Tantalus Cocktail

⅓ Forbidden Fruit Liqueur, ⅓ Cognac, ⅓ Lemon Juice. Shake and strain.

Tempter Cocktail

½ Port Wine, ½ Apricot Liqueur. Stir and strain.

Texas Fizz

1 teaspoonful of sugar, juice of 1 lemon and 1 orange, 2 ounces of Gin. Shake well, pour into tumbler and add Soda Water.

Texas Rose

⅓ Bourbon, ⅔ Orange Juice, 1 dash Cherry Liqueur. Shake well and strain. Top off with Champagne.
(Recipe: Philippe Recher, Paris, 1973.)

Third Degree Cocktail

⅔ Gin, ⅓ Dry Vermouth, 4 dashes of Absinthe. Shake and strain over ice in small tumbler.

Three Mile Limit Cocktail

3 dashes of Grenadine, 2 dashes of Lemon Juice, ⅔ Cognac, ⅓ Bacardi Rum. Shake and strain.
(Recipe: 'Chips' Brighton, Harry's Bar, Paris, 1925.)

Thunder Cocktail

Pinch of sugar, 1 yolk of egg, 2 ounces of Cognac, 1 sprinkle of Cayenne Pepper, 1 dash of Tabasco. Shake well and strain.

Tiger's Milk Cocktail

⅓ Cognac, ⅓ Cointreau, ⅓ Kahlua, fresh cream. Shake well, pour into tall tumbler with ice, decorate with fruit.
(Recipe: Harry's Bar, Munich, 1975.)

Tlevesoor Cocktail

1 dash each of Peach Bitters, Holland Gin, Curaçao, ⅙ Orange Juice, ⅙ Grapefruit Juice, ⅓ Rye Whiskey, ⅓ Calvados. Shake well and strain.
(Recipe: Bob Card, Harry's Bar, Paris. 4th March, 1933: for the inauguration of President Roosevelt.)

Tom and Jerry (hot)

Use eggs according to quantity. Take bowl and break up your eggs very carefully without mixing the yolks with the whites, but have the whites in a separate bowl. Take an egg-beater and beat the whites to a stiff froth, then beat the yolks until they are as thin as water. Now mix all together, adding one teaspoonful of sugar for each egg, until the mixture has the consistency of a light batter. It is necessary to stir up the mixture every little while to prevent the eggs from separating. Use tumbler or tankard and take 2 tablespoonfuls of the above mixture, 1 ounce of Cognac, 1 ounce of Jamaica Rum. Complete with boiling water or milk, according to taste, and stir up well. Then pour from one tumbler to another, until all ingredients are thoroughly mixed together. Grate a little nutmeg on top and serve.

Tom and Jerry (cold)

Same as Hot Tom and Jerry, but use ice-cold milk or water.

Tom Collins

In large tumbler: ice, juice of lemon, 2 ounces of Gin. Fill balance with Soda Water, serve.

Tomate Cocktail

In tall tumbler: ice, 1 spoonful of Grenadine, 2 ounces of Pernod, water to taste.

Torpedo

In short tumbler: pack crushed ice, 2 ounces of Southern Comfort. Float 1 ounce of 120 Proof Malt Whisky, serve with short straws.
(Recipe: John Bruno, NY, Pen and Pencil Restaurant.)

Trilby Cocktail

2 dashes of Anis and 2 of Orange Bitters, ⅓ Parfait Amour Liqueur, ⅓ Scotch Whisky, ⅓ Sweet Vermouth. Shake and strain.

Trinity Cocktail

⅓ Dry Vermouth, ⅓ Sweet Vermouth, ⅓ Gin. Stir and serve.

Tropical Cocktail

1 dash of Angostura, Orange Bitters, ⅓ Crème de Cacao, ⅓ Maraschino, ⅓ Dry Martini Vermouth. Stir well and strain, with cherry.

Twelve Miles Out Cocktail

⅓ Light Rum, ⅓ Swedish Punsch, ⅓ Calvados. Stir and strain, twist orange peel.

Veronique Cocktail

In tumbler: ice, 1 spoonful of Crème de Cassis, 2 ounces of Calvados. Complete with Cider.

Vie en Rose Cocktail

⅙ Lemon Juice, ⅙ Grenadine, ⅓ Gin, ⅓ Kirschwasser. Shake and strain.

Virgin Cocktail

⅓ Forbidden Fruit Liqueur, ⅓ White Crème de Menthe, ⅓ Gin. Shake and strain.

Viva Zapata

In large tumbler: ice, 2 ounces of Mescal, juice of one lemon, fill up with Soda.

Vodkatini Cocktail

⁹⁄₁₀ Vodka, ¹⁄₁₀ Dry Vermouth. Stir and serve.

Volstead Cocktail

⅓ Rye Whiskey, ⅓ Swedish Punsch, ⅙ Orange Juice, ⅙ Raspberry Syrup, 1 dash of Anisette.
(Recipe: This cocktail was invented at Harry's Bar, Paris, in honour of Mr Andrew J. Volstead (who brought out the Dry Act in the USA) and was the reason for sending such a large number of Americans to Europe to quench their thirst.)

Wanda's Dream Cocktail

⅓ Grand Marnier, ⅓ Gin, ⅓ Sweet Martini Vermouth. Stir and strain.

Ward Eight

½ Rye Whiskey, ¼ Orange Juice, ¼ Lemon Juice, 4 dashes of Grenadine. Shake and strain.

Warday's Cocktail

1 teaspoonful of Yellow Chartreuse, ⅓ Sweet Vermouth, ⅓ Gin, ⅓ Calvados. Shake and strain.

Wax Cocktail

1 white of egg, 1 teaspoonful of Gomme Syrup, ½ Gin, ½ Absinthe or Anis. Shake and strain.

Welcome Stranger Cocktail

⅙ Grenadine, ⅙ Lemon Juice, ⅙ Gin, ⅙ Swedish Punsch, ⅙ Orange Juice, ⅙ Cognac. Shake and strain.
(Recipe: Harry MacElhone, Harry's Bar, Paris, 1934.)

Whiskey Sour

In shaker: 2 ounces of Bourbon Whiskey, juice of ½ a lemon, sugar to taste. Shake and strain, decorate with cherry.

White Bird

In shaker: ice, ⅔ Bourbon Whiskey, ⅙ Banana Liqueur, ⅙ fresh cream. Shake and strain in cocktail glass.
(Recipe: François, Harry's Bar, Munich, 1985.)

White Lady Cocktail

⅓ Lemon Juice, ⅓ White Crème de Menthe, ⅓ Cointreau. Shake well and strain.
(Recipe: This was the original brought out by Harry MacElhone at Ciro's Club in London in 1919. He later changed it to: ⅓ Gin, ⅓ Cointreau, ⅓ Lemon Juice, at Harry's Bar, Paris, 1929.)

White Russian Cocktail

½ Vodka, ½ Kahlua. Shake well, or pour directly on the rocks, and cover top with fresh cream.

Whoopee Cocktail

In large champagne glass: 1 lump of ice, ½ Curaçao, ½ Cognac. Fill balance with Champagne.

Winter Sunshine Cocktail

⅔ Gin, ⅓ Cointreau, 3 dashes of Scotch. Stir and strain.
(Recipe: Andy MacElhone, Harry's Bar, Paris, 1958.)

Woon Fizz

2 ounces of Gin, juice of 1 lemon, sugar to taste, 4 dashes of Anis. Shake well and strain in small tumbler, add Soda Water.
(Recipe: Mr Basil Woon, author of The Frantic Atlantic, *Paris, 1929.)*

Xanthia Cocktail

⅓ Cherry Brandy, ⅓ Yellow Chartreuse, ⅓ Gin.
Shake well and strain.

XYZ Cocktail

½ Rum, ¼ Cointreau, ¼ Lemon Juice. Shake
well and strain.

Yale Cocktail

3 dashes of Orange Bitters, 1 dash of Angostura, 2 ounces of Gin, ice, lemon peel, in medium-sized tumbler, add Soda Water.

Yellow Boxer

½ Tequila, ½ Lime Juice Cordial, 4 dashes of Galliano. Shake well and strain.

Yellow Daisy

½ Gin, ¼ Dry Vermouth, ¼ Grand Marnier. Stir and serve.

Yokohama Cocktail

1 dash of Anis, ⅙ Grenadine, ⅙ Orange Juice, ⅓ Vodka, ⅓ Gin. Shake and strain.

Yo-Yo

⅖ Calvados, ⅕ Cherry Brandy, ⅖ Pineapple Juice. Shake well and strain.

Zagorian Special

In shaker: ice, ⅓ Safari Liqueur, ⅔ Cognac, fresh cream and Pineapple Juice to taste. Shake and serve in tumbler with the ice.
(Recipe: S. Zagori, Harry's Bar, Paris, 1983.)

Zaza Cocktail

1 dash of Angostura, ½ Gin, ½ Dubonnet. Stir and serve.

Zombie Cocktail

In very tall tumbler: 1 ounce of Jamaica Rum, 1 ounce of Light Rum, ¼ ounce of Cointreau. Add equal parts of Lime Juice, Orange Juice, Pineapple Juice, 2 dashes of Grenadine. Stir and decorate with fruit, float 151 Proof Rum on top.

Zoom Cocktail

2 ounces of Cognac, 1 tablespoonful of honey and of fresh cream. Shake well, strain into small tumbler.

INDEX OF COCKTAILS

101